soups

p

This is a Parragon Book
First published in 2002

Parragon
Queen Street House
4 Queen Street
Bath BA1 1HE
United Kingdom

Copyright © Parragon 2002

All rights reserved. No part of this publication may be reproduced, stored in a
retrieval system or transmitted, in any form or by any means, electronic,
mechanical, photocopying, recording or otherwise, without the prior permission
of the copyright holder.

ISBN: 0-75258-008-6

Printed in Spain

Produced by The Bridgewater Book Company Ltd, Lewes, East Sussex

Acknowledgements
Creative Director Terry Jeavons
Art Director Sarah Howerd
Editorial Director Fiona Biggs
Senior Editor Mark Truman
Editorial Assistants Simon Bailey, Tom Kitch
Page Make-up Sara Kidd

NOTES FOR THE READER

- This book uses both metric and imperial measurements. Follow the same units of measurement throughout; do not mix metric and imperial.
- All spoon measurements are level: teaspoons are assumed to be 5 ml, and table-spoons are assumed to be 15 ml.
- Unless otherwise stated, milk is assumed to be full-fat, eggs and individual vegetables such as potatoes are medium-sized, and pepper is freshly ground black pepper.
- Recipes using raw or very lightly cooked eggs should be avoided by infants, the elderly, pregnant women, convalescents, and anyone suffering from an illness.
- Optional ingredients, variations, and serving suggestions have not been included in the calculations.
- The times given are an approximate guide only. Preparation times differ according to the techniques used by different people and the cooking times vary as a result of the type of oven used.

Contents

Introduction   4

Light Soups   6

Hearty Soups   40

Special Occasions   76

Index   96

Introduction

A soup may be thick and nourishing, as substantial as a light meal. Soups are traditionally a winter food, and indeed, Provençal Pumpkin Winter soup is very warming. Yet Spinach Soup is one example of a light soup, and Prawn Bisque with Rice is elegant enough to present as the first course at a formal dinner party. In fact, soups provide endless gastronomic scope. There are hot, spicy soups such as Chicken, Avocado & Chipotle soup from Mexico, and others from India and Thailand. Greek Egg and Lemon soup is a refreshing fruit-flavoured soup for warmer days, and cold soups, such Melon Gazpacho and Cucumber and Smoked Salmon, are chilled soups for hot days.

Soup is easy to prepare and cook, but to be delicious it must be based on a well-flavoured stock, usually a vegetable stock or one based on chicken or beef. It is best to make your own or to

guide to recipe key	
easy	Recipes are graded as follows: 1 pea = easy; 2 peas = very easy; 3 peas = extremely easy.
serves 4	Most of the recipes in this book serve four people. Simply halve the ingredients to serve two, taking care not to mix imperial and metric measurements.
15 minutes	Preparation time. Where recipes include time for chilling or standing, these are listed separately: eg, 15 minutes, plus 30 minutes to chill.
40 minutes	Cooking time. Where recipes include time for standing before serving, this will be listed: eg, 40 minutes, plus 10 minutes to cool.

use ready-made fresh or frozen stock, but for convenience and speed, good-quality stock cubes or powder are an essential ingredient for the kitchen cupboard along with many of the staple ingredients used in soups: rice, barley, and other grains, dried pulses, pasta and noodles, herbs and spices. Almost any food can be the star ingredient in a soup – vegetables, meat, poultry, fish and seafood, beans, pasta, or fruit – as the recipes in this book show. The secret of a distinctive soup is to add herbs and spices, and to use appropriate cooking techniques to draw out the character of the main ingredients.

Chicken, Avocado & Chipotle Soup, page 88

Light Soups

A light soup, garnished with fresh herbs or perhaps a swirl of cream, is the perfect opener to a formal meal, especially if you are planning to follow it with a fairly hearty main course and a very rich dessert. A stylish classic soup is Prawn Bisque with Rice, made special by the addition of brandy and white wine; while Sweet Potato, Apple & Leek Soup has a pretty colour and an unusual ingredient – apple juice. Chilled Garlic and Almond Soup is a cold soup for a hot summer lunch, with an unusual combination of flavours.

Spicy Gazpacho

1 cucumber
2 green peppers
6 ripe tomatoes
½ fresh hot chilli
½–1 onion, chopped
  finely
3–4 garlic cloves,
  chopped
4 tbsp extra-virgin
  olive oil
¼–½ tsp ground cumin
2–4 tsp sherry vinegar,
  or a combination of
  balsamic vinegar and
  wine vinegar
4 tbsp chopped fresh
  coriander
2 tbsp chopped fresh
  parsley
300 ml/10 fl oz vegetable
  or chicken stock
600 ml/1 pint tomato
  juice or canned
  crushed tomatoes
salt and pepper
ice cubes, to serve

❶ Cut the cucumber in half lengthways, then cut it into quarters. Remove the seeds with a teaspoon, then dice the flesh. Cut the peppers in half, remove the cores and seeds, then dice the flesh. Add to the chopped onion in the bowl.

❷ To skin the fresh tomatoes, place them in a heat-resistant bowl, pour boiling water over to cover them, and leave for 30 seconds. Drain and plunge into cold water. The skins will then slide off easily. Cut the tomatoes in half, deseed, and chop the flesh. Deseed and chop the chilli.

❸ Combine half the cucumber, green pepper, tomatoes and onion in a blender or a food processor with all the chilli, garlic, olive oil, cumin, vinegar, coriander and parsley. Process with enough stock to make a smooth purée.

❹ Pour the puréed soup into a bowl and stir in the remaining stock and tomato juice. Add the remaining green pepper, cucumber, tomatoes and onion, stirring well. Season with salt and pepper to taste, then cover and chill for at least 2 hours.

❺ Ladle into bowls and serve with ice cubes in each bowl.

❷

❹

❹

very easy

serves 4

20 minutes,
plus 2 hours
to chill

0 minutes

8

Spicy Courgette Soup with Rice & Lime

INGREDIENTS

2 tbsp oil
4 garlic cloves,
    sliced thinly
1–2 tbsp mild red
    chilli powder
¼–½ tsp ground cumin
1.5 litres/2¾ pints
    chicken, vegetable
    or beef stock
2 courgettes, cut into
    bite-sized chunks
4 tbsp long-grain rice
salt and pepper
fresh oregano sprigs,
    to garnish
lime wedges, to serve
    (optional)

❶ Heat the oil in a heavy-based pan, add the garlic, and fry for about 2 minutes, or until softened and just beginning to change colour. Add the chilli powder and cumin, and cook over a medium–low heat for 1 minute.

❷ Stir in the stock, courgettes and rice, bring just to the boil, then cook over a medium–high heat for about 10 minutes, or until the courgettes are just tender and the rice is cooked through. Season the soup with salt and pepper.

❸ Ladle into soup bowls, garnish with oregano sprigs, and serve with lime wedges.

 extremely easy

serves 4

 5 minutes

15 minutes

COOK'S TIP
Courgettes should be firm to the touch and have shiny skin. The younger ones have the best flavour, so they should be small.

Prawn Bisque with Rice

INGREDIENTS

650 g/1 lb 7 oz cooked prawns, in their shell
1 stick of celery with leaves, chopped
½ tsp crushed dried chillies
about 1.2 litres/2 pints water
60 g/2¼ oz butter
1 onion, chopped finely
2 carrots, chopped finely
50 ml/2 fl oz brandy or Cognac
225 ml/8 fl oz dry white wine
1 bay leaf and 10 parsley sprigs, tied together with kitchen string
1–2 tsp tomato purée
1 tsp paprika
3 tbsp basmati or long-grain white rice
150 ml/5 fl oz double or whipping cream
fresh dill sprigs or long chives, to garnish

❶ Peel 6 prawns, leaving the tails intact, and set aside for garnishing. Peel the remaining prawns, reserving the shells.

❷ Put all the shells in a saucepan with the stick of celery and dried chillies. Add the water. Bring to the boil over a high heat, skimming off any foam. Reduce the heat and simmer for 30 minutes. Strain and set the stock aside.

❸ Melt the butter in a large saucepan. Add the onion and carrots, and cook for about 8 minutes, stirring frequently, until the vegetables are soft. Add the brandy and, standing well back, ignite with a long match. Allow the flames to die down, then stir in the wine. Boil for about 5 minutes to reduce by about half.

❹ Add the reserved stock, bay leaf and parsley stem bundle, tomato purée, paprika and rice. Stir to combine. Bring to the boil, then simmer gently for 20 minutes, or until the rice is very tender.

❺ Remove the parsley bundle. Working in batches if necessary, process the soup in a blender and strain into a clean saucepan. Stir in the cream and simmer for about 2 minutes. Add the 6 prawns and heat through for 1 minute. Ladle into 6 bowls, arranging a prawn in each serving. Garnish the soup with dill sprigs or chives, and serve.

easy

serves 6

15 minutes

1 hour,
20 minutes

Greek Egg & Lemon Soup

INGREDIENTS

1.5 litres/2¾ pints
   chicken or lamb stock
75–100 g/2¾–3½ oz
   long-grain white rice
3 eggs, separated
3–4 tbsp lemon juice
1 tbsp water
salt and white pepper
1 tbsp chopped fresh
   flat-leaved parsley, to
   garnish (optional)

easy

serves 4

30 minutes

30 minutes

❶ Bring the stock to the boil in a large saucepan. Add the rice in a very slow stream so that the stock does not stop boiling. Stir once or twice. Reduce the heat and simmer gently, partially covered, until the rice is tender. Skim off any foam that rises to the surface.

❷ Whisk the egg whites in a large bowl until almost stiff.

❸ Add the egg yolks and continue whisking until the mixture is light and creamy. Beat in the lemon juice and water a little at a time.

❹ Whisk in half of the hot stock and the rice gradually, about 2 tablespoons at a time. Be careful to add the hot stock very slowly to the egg and lemon mixture, and whisk constantly, otherwise the eggs may curdle (see Cook's Tip).

❺ Remove the remaining stock and rice from the heat, transfer to a bowl and gradually whisk in the egg and stock mixture. Continue to whisk for 1 minute to allow the stock to cool slightly. Season the soup with salt and pepper, and serve it immediately, perhaps garnished with a little chopped parsley.

COOK'S TIP

To prevent curdling, pour the egg whites into a food processor fitted with the metal blade. Process until thick and foamy, add the yolks, and process for 1 minute. With the machine running, add the lemon and water slowly until combined. Continue from Step 4.

❷  ❹  ❺

Chilled Garlic & Almond Soup

INGREDIENTS

400 g/14 oz day-old
   French bread, sliced
4 large garlic cloves
3–4 tbsp sherry vinegar
1 litre/1¾ pints water,
   chilled
6 tbsp extra-virgin
   olive oil
225 g/8 oz ground
   almonds
sea salt and pepper

TO GARNISH
seedless white grapes,
   chilled and sliced
pepper
extra-virgin olive oil

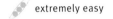 extremely easy

 serves 4

25–30 minutes,
plus 4 hours
to chill

0 minutes

COOK'S TIP
The traditional accompaniment to this soup is chilled grapes, but garlic-lovers might prefer to sprinkle thin slices of garlic fried in olive oil until golden brown over the soup.

❶ Tear the bread into small pieces and put it in a bowl. Pour over enough cold water to cover the bread and leave to soak for 10–15 minutes. Using your hands, squeeze the bread dry. Transfer the bread to a food processor.

❷ Cut the garlic cloves in half lengthways and use the tip of the knife to remove the pale green or white cores. Add the garlic and 3 tablespoons of the sherry vinegar to the food processor with 225 ml/8 fl oz of the water, then process until blended. Add the oil and ground almonds, and blend.

❸ With the motor running, pour in the remaining water slowly until a smooth soup forms. Add extra sherry vinegar to taste, and season with salt and pepper. Transfer to a bowl, cover, and chill for at least 4 hours.

❹ Ladle into bowls and float grapes on top. Garnish each bowl with a sprinkling of pepper and a swirl of olive oil. Serve while still cold.

16

Roasted Pepper & Tomato Soup with Dill

INGREDIENTS

1 kg/2 lb 4 oz juicy plum tomatoes, halved

2 large red peppers, cored, deseeded and halved

1 onion, quartered

3 sprigs fresh dill, tied together, plus a little extra to garnish

1 thin piece of orange rind

juice of 1 orange

600 ml/1 pint vegetable stock

1–1½ tbsp red wine vinegar

salt and pepper

any bread typical of the Mediterranean region, to serve

 very easy

 serves 4

 15 minutes

1 hour

COOK'S TIP

A food mill, or mouli-legume as it is called in France, is ideal for puréeing vegetable soups and sauces because it removes the skin and seeds.

❶ Place the tomatoes and peppers on a baking sheet, cut-sides up to catch the juices. Add the onion quarters. Place in a preheated oven at 230°C/450°F/Gas Mark 8 and roast for 20–25 minutes, or until the vegetables just start to char on the edges.

❷ As the vegetables become charred, transfer them to a large flameproof casserole or a stockpot. Add the dill, orange rind and juice, stock, and salt and pepper to taste. Bring to the boil.

❸ Lower the heat, partially cover, and simmer the soup for 25 minutes. Remove the bundle of dill and transfer the rest of the ingredients to a food mill (see Cook's Tip), then purée. Alternatively, process the soup in a food processor and work it through a fine sieve.

❹ Return the soup to the rinsed casserole or stockpot, and reheat. Stir in the vinegar and adjust the seasoning with salt and pepper, if necessary. Ladle into bowls and garnish with extra dill. Serve hot, with hunks or slices of a bread of the Mediterranean region.

Spinach Soup

INGREDIENTS

1 tbsp olive oil
1 onion, halved and
    sliced thinly
1 leek, split lengthways
    and sliced thinly
1 potato, diced finely
1 litre/1¾ pints water
2 sprigs fresh marjoram
    or ¼ tsp dried
2 sprigs fresh thyme or
    ¼ tsp dried
1 bay leaf
400 g/14 oz young
    spinach, washed
freshly grated nutmeg
salt and pepper
4 tbsp single cream,
    to serve

❶ Heat the oil in a heavy-based saucepan over a medium heat. Add the onion and leek and cook for about 3 minutes, stirring occasionally, until they begin to soften.

❷ Add the potato, water, marjoram, thyme and bay leaf, with a large pinch of salt. Bring to the boil, reduce the heat, cover, and cook gently for 25 minutes, or until the vegetables are tender. Remove the bay leaf and the herb stems.

❸ Add the spinach and continue cooking for 3–4 minutes, stirring frequently, until it is completely wilted.

❹ Allow the soup to cool slightly, then transfer to a blender or a food processor and purée until smooth, working in batches if necessary. (If using a food processor, strain off the cooking liquid and reserve. Purée the soup solids with enough cooking liquid to moisten them, then combine with the remaining liquid.)

❺ Return the soup to the saucepan and thin it with a little more water, if wished. Season with salt, a good grinding of pepper and a generous grating of nutmeg. Place the pan over a low heat and simmer until reheated.

❻ Ladle the soup into warm bowls and swirl a tablespoon of cream into each serving.

 very easy

 serves 4

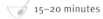 15–20 minutes

50 minutes

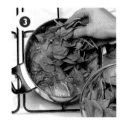

Celeriac, Leek & Potato Soup

INGREDIENTS

1 tbsp butter
1 onion, chopped
2 large leeks, halved
    lengthways and sliced
1 large celeriac (about
    750 g/1 lb 10 oz),
    peeled and cubed
1 potato, cubed
1 carrot, quartered and
    sliced thinly
1.2 litres/2 pints water
⅛ tsp dried marjoram
1 bay leaf
freshly grated nutmeg
salt and pepper
celery leaves, to garnish

❶ Melt the butter in a large saucepan over a medium–low heat. Add the onion and leeks to the pan, and cook for about 4 minutes, stirring frequently, until just softened, but do not allow them to colour.

❷ Add the celeriac, potato, carrot, water, marjoram and bay leaf, with a large pinch of salt. Bring to the boil, reduce the heat, cover, and simmer for about 25 minutes, or until the vegetables are tender. Remove the bay leaf.

❸ Allow the soup to cool slightly. Transfer to a blender or a food processor and purée until smooth. (If using a food processor, strain off the cooking liquid and reserve. Purée the soup solids with enough cooking liquid to moisten them, then combine with the remaining liquid.)

❹ Return the puréed soup to the saucepan and stir to blend. Season with salt, pepper and nutmeg. Simmer over a medium–low heat until reheated.

❺ Ladle the soup into warm bowls, garnish with celery leaves, and serve at once.

very easy

serves 4

15 minutes

45 minutes

Tarragon Pea Soup

INGREDIENTS

2 tsp butter
1 onion, chopped finely
2 leeks, chopped finely
75 g/2¾ oz white rice
500 g/1 lb 2 oz frozen
*   peas*
1 litre/1¾ pints water
1 chicken or vegetable
*   stock cube*
¾ tsp dried tarragon
salt and pepper
chopped hard-boiled
*   egg or croûtons,*
*   to garnish*

very easy

serves 4

10–15 minutes

1 hour, 5 minutes

❶ Melt the butter in a large saucepan over a medium–low heat. Add the onion, leeks and rice. Cover and cook for about 10 minutes, stirring occasionally, until the vegetables are softened.

❷ Add the peas, water, stock cube and tarragon, and bring just to the boil. Season with a little pepper. Cover, and simmer for about 35 minutes, stirring occasionally, until the vegetables are very tender.

❸ Allow the soup to cool slightly, then transfer to a blender or a food processor and purée until smooth, working in batches if necessary. (If using a food processor, strain off the cooking liquid and reserve. Purée the soup solids with enough cooking liquid to moisten them, then combine with the remaining liquid.)

❹ Return the puréed soup to the saucepan. Taste and adjust the seasoning, adding plenty of pepper and, if needed, salt. Gently reheat the soup over a low heat for about 10 minutes, or until hot.

❺ Ladle into warm bowls and garnish with egg or croûtons.

COOK'S TIP
The rice gives the soup a little extra body, but a small amount of raw or cooked potato would do the same job.

Sweet Potato, Apple & Leek Soup

1 tbsp butter
3 leeks, sliced thinly
1 large carrot,
    sliced thinly
2 sweet potatoes,
    peeled and cubed
2 large tart eating
    apples, peeled and
    cubed
1.2 litres/2 pints water
freshly grated nutmeg
225 ml/8 fl oz apple juice
225 ml/8 fl oz whipping
    or single cream
salt and pepper
snipped fresh chives or
    fresh coriander leaves,
    to garnish

❶ Melt the butter in a large saucepan over a medium–low heat. Add the leeks, cover, and cook for 6–8 minutes, or until softened, stirring frequently.

❷ Add the carrot, sweet potatoes, apples and water. Season lightly with salt, pepper and nutmeg. Bring to the boil, reduce the heat, and simmer, covered, for about 20 minutes, stirring occasionally, until the vegetables are very tender.

❸ Allow the soup to cool slightly, then transfer to a blender or a food processor and purée until smooth, working in batches if necessary. (If using a food processor, strain off the cooking liquid and reserve. Purée the soup solids with enough cooking liquid to moisten them, then combine with the remaining liquid.)

❹ Return the puréed soup to the saucepan and stir in the apple juice. Place over a low heat and simmer for about 10 minutes, or until heated through.

❺ Stir in the cream and continue simmering for about 5 minutes, stirring frequently, until heated through. Taste and adjust the seasoning, adding more salt, pepper and nutmeg, if necessary. Ladle the soup into warm bowls, garnish with chives or coriander, and serve.

very easy

serves 4

15 minutes

1 hour

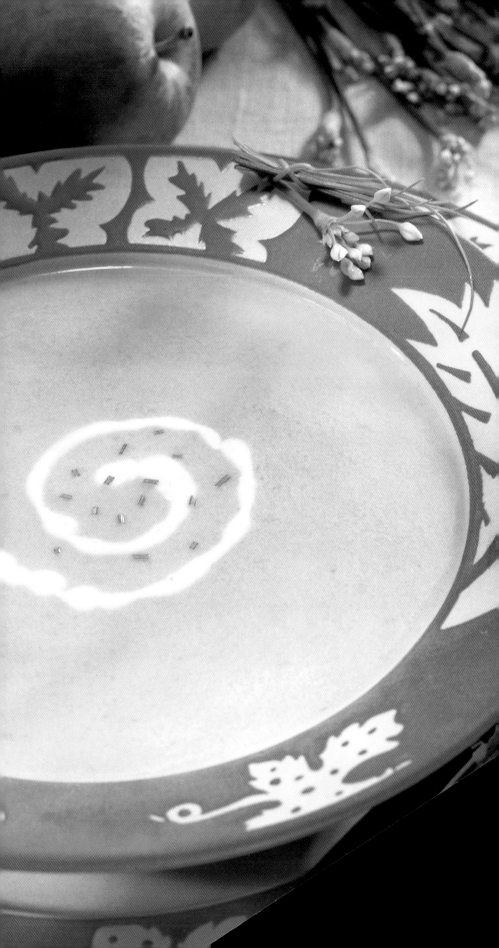

Chicken Soup with Stars

INGREDIENTS

75 g/2¾ oz small pasta stars, or other very small shapes
chopped fresh parsley

CHICKEN STOCK
1.25 kg/2 lb 12 oz chicken pieces, such as wings or legs
2.5 litres/4½ pints water
1 stick of celery, sliced
1 large carrot, sliced
1 onion, sliced
1 leek, sliced
2 garlic cloves, crushed
8 peppercorns
4 allspice berries
3–4 parsley sprigs
2–3 fresh thyme sprigs
1 bay leaf
½ tsp salt
pepper

❶ Put the chicken in a large 4 litre/7 pint pot with the water, celery, carrot, onion, leek, garlic, peppercorns, allspice, herbs and salt. Bring just to the boil and skim off the foam that rises to the surface. Reduce the heat and simmer, partially covered, for 2 hours.

❷ Remove the chicken from the stock and set aside to cool. Continue simmering the stock, uncovered, for about 30 minutes. When the chicken is cool enough to handle, remove the meat from the bones and, if necessary, cut into bite-sized pieces.

❸ Strain the stock and remove as much fat as possible. Discard the vegetables and flavourings. (There should be about 1.7 litres/3 pints of chicken stock.)

❹ Bring the stock to the boil in a clean saucepan. Add the pasta and regulate the heat so that the stock boils very gently. Cook for about 10 minutes, or until the pasta is tender, but still firm to the bite.

❺ Stir in the chicken meat. Taste the soup and adjust the seasoning. Ladle into warm bowls and serve sprinkled with parsley.

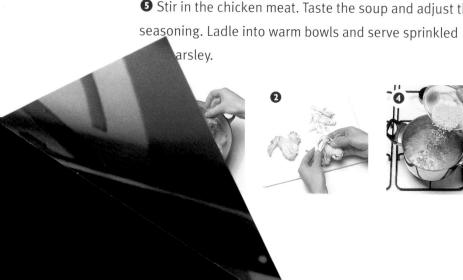

Melon Gazpacho

INGREDIENTS

1 tsp oil
1 onion, chopped finely
1 large garlic clove,
    chopped finely
1 tsp chopped fresh chilli
700 g/1 lb 9 oz seedless
    Cantaloupe melon
    flesh, cubed
½ tsp raspberry vinegar,
    or 1 tsp lemon juice
pinch of salt
½ ripe green melon, such
    as Galia (about 500 g/
    1 lb 2 oz)
snipped chives,
    to garnish

extremely easy

serves 4

15 minutes,
plus 30 minutes
to chill

8 minutes

❶ Heat the oil in a small pan over a low heat. Add the onion, garlic and chilli, cover, and cook for 6–7 minutes, stirring occasionally, until the onion is soft but not browned.

❷ Put the Cantaloupe melon flesh in a blender or a food processor, add the onion, garlic and chilli mixture, and purée until smooth, stopping to scrape down the sides as necessary. (You may need to work in batches.) Add the vinegar or lemon juice with the salt, and process to combine.

❸ Chill for about 30 minutes, or until the mixture is cold.

❹ Remove the seeds from the green melon, then cut it into balls with a melon baller. Alternatively, cut it into cubes with a sharp knife.

❺ Divide the soup among 4 shallow bowls and top with the green melon balls. Sprinkle lightly with chives to garnish, and serve the soup cold.

COOK'S TIP

If you are wary of using fresh chilli, omit it and add a few drops of hot pepper sauce to taste, at the end of Step 2, to liven up the soup.

Watercress Vichyssoise

INGREDIENTS

1 tbsp olive oil
3 large leeks, sliced
thinly (about
350 g/12 oz)
1 large potato, diced
finely (about
350 g/12 oz)
600 ml/1 pint chicken
or vegetable stock
450 ml/16 fl oz water
1 bay leaf
175 g/6 oz prepared
watercress
200 ml/7 fl oz single
cream
salt and pepper
watercress leaves,
to garnish

❶ Heat the oil in a heavy-based saucepan over a medium heat. Add the leeks and cook for about 3 minutes, stirring frequently, until they begin to soften.

❷ Add the potato, stock, water and bay leaf. Add salt if the stock is unsalted. Bring to the boil, reduce the heat, cover and cook gently for 25 minutes, or until the vegetables are tender. It may be difficult to find the bay leaf, but it is best removed at this point.

❸ Add the watercress and cook for another 2–3 minutes, stirring frequently, until the watercress is wilted completely.

❹ Allow the soup to cool slightly, then transfer to a blender or a food processor and purée until smooth. Work in batches if necessary. (If using a food processor, strain off the liquid and reserve. Purée the soup solids with enough liquid to moisten them, then combine with the remaining liquid.)

❺ Put the soup in a large bowl and stir in half the cream. Season with salt, if needed, and plenty of pepper.

❻ Refrigerate until cold. Taste and adjust the seasoning, if necessary. Ladle into chilled bowls, drizzle the remaining cream on top, and garnish the soup with watercress leaves. Serve at once.

very easy

serves 4

15–20 minutes,
plus 2–3 hours
to chill

50 minutes

Cold Cucumber
& Smoked Salmon Soup

INGREDIENTS

2 tsp oil
1 large onion, chopped
*   finely*
1 large cucumber, peeled,
*   deseeded and sliced*
1 small potato, diced
1 stick of celery, chopped
*   finely*
1 litre/1¾ pints chicken
*   or vegetable stock*
150 ml/5 fl oz double
*   cream*
150 g/5½ oz smoked
*   salmon, diced finely*
2 tbsp chopped fresh
*   chives*
salt and pepper
fresh dill sprigs,
*   to garnish*

❶ Heat the oil in a large saucepan over a medium heat. Add the onion and cook for about 3 minutes, or until it begins to soften.

❷ Add the cucumber, potato, celery and stock, with a large pinch of salt if you are using unsalted stock. Bring to the boil, reduce the heat, then cover the pan, and cook gently for about 20 minutes, or until the vegetables are tender.

❸ Allow the soup to cool slightly, then transfer to a blender or a food processor, working in batches if necessary.

❹ Purée the soup until smooth. If using a food processor, strain off the cooking liquid and reserve it. Purée the soup solids with enough cooking liquid to moisten them, then combine with the remaining liquid.

❺ Transfer the puréed soup into a large container. Cover, and refrigerate until cold.

❻ Stir the cream, salmon and chives into the soup. If time permits, chill for at least 1 hour to allow the flavours to blend. Taste and adjust the seasoning, adding salt, if needed, and pepper. Ladle into chilled bowls and garnish with fresh dill sprigs.

very easy

serves 4

25 minutes,
plus 1 hour
to chill

35 minutes

Mushroom & Tofu Broth

INGREDIENTS

4 dried black mushrooms
1 tbsp sunflower oil
1 tsp sesame oil
1 garlic clove, crushed
1 green chilli, deseeded
*   and chopped finely*
6 spring onions
85 g/3 oz fresh oyster
*   mushrooms, sliced*
2 kaffir lime leaves,
*   shredded finely*
1 litre/1¾ pints rich
*   brown stock*
2 tbsp lime juice
1 tbsp rice vinegar
1 tbsp Thai fish sauce
85 g/3 oz firm tofu, diced
salt and pepper

❶ Pour 150 ml/5 fl oz boiling water over the dried black mushrooms in a heatproof bowl and leave to soak for about 30 minutes. Drain, reserving the liquid, then chop the black mushrooms roughly.

❷ Heat the sunflower and sesame oils in a large pan or a wok over a high heat. Add the garlic, chilli and spring onions, and stir for 1 minute, or until softened but not browned.

❸ Add all of the mushrooms, kaffir lime leaves, stock and reserved mushroom liquid. Bring to the boil.

❹ Stir in the lime juice, rice vinegar and fish sauce, lower the heat, and simmer gently for 3–4 minutes.

❺ Add the diced tofu and adjust the seasoning to taste with salt and pepper. Heat gently until the soup is boiling, then serve immediately.

 extremely easy

 serves 4

 10 minutes,
plus 30 minutes
to soak

25 minutes

Sweet & Sour Cabbage Soup

INGREDIENTS

85 g/3 oz sultanas
125 ml/4 fl oz orange
juice
1 tbsp olive oil
1 large onion, chopped
250 g/9 oz shredded
cabbage
2 apples, peeled and
diced
125 ml/4 fl oz apple juice
400 g/14 oz canned
peeled tomatoes
in juice
225 ml/8 fl oz tomato
or vegetable juice
100 g/3½ oz pineapple
flesh, chopped finely
1.2 litres/2 pints water
2 tsp wine vinegar
salt and pepper
fresh mint leaves,
to garnish

❶ Put the sultanas in a bowl, pour the orange juice over them, and leave for 15 minutes.

❷ Heat the oil in a large saucepan over a medium heat, add the onion, cover, and cook for 3–4 minutes, stirring frequently, until it starts to soften. Add the cabbage and cook for another 2 minutes without allowing it to brown.

❸ Add the apples and apple juice, cover, and cook gently for 5 minutes. Stir in the tomatoes, tomato juice, pineapple and water. Season to taste and add the vinegar.

❹ Add the sultanas with their soaking liquid. Bring to the boil, reduce the heat and simmer, partially covered, for 1 hour, or until the fruit and vegetables are tender.

❺ Allow the soup to cool slightly, then transfer to a blender or a food processor and purée until smooth, working in batches if necessary. (If using a food processor, strain off the liquid and reserve. Purée the solids with enough liquid to moisten them, then combine with the remaining liquid.)

❻ Return the soup to the saucepan and simmer gently for about 10 minutes to reheat. Ladle into warm bowls. Garnish with mint leaves and serve immediately.

 very easy

serves 4

15 minutes,
plus 15 minutes
to stand

1½ hours

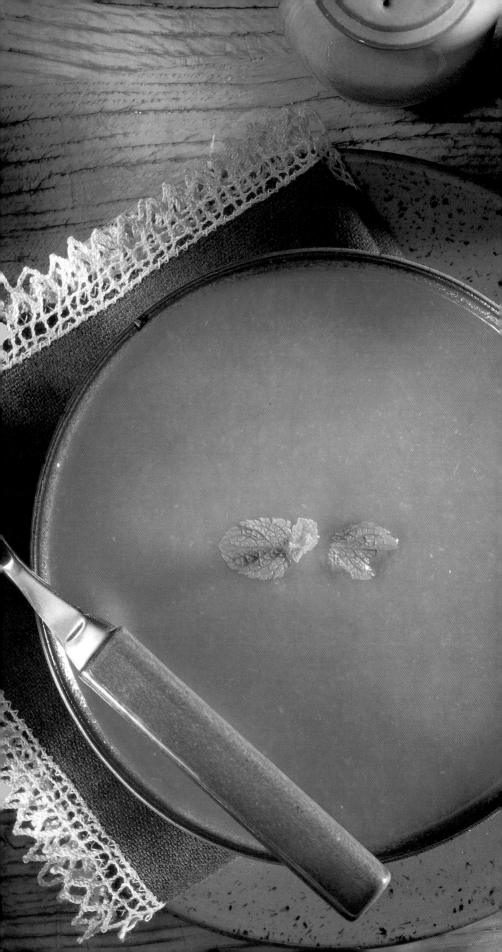

Hearty Soups

These thick soups all make a cheering fast lunch during a busy working day. Barley & Rice Soup with Chard is so thick it is almost a vegetarian stew. Beef & Vegetable soup and Pozole from Mexico, made with pork and chicken, need only 10 minutes' preparation time and can be left to simmer until ready. Hearty soups are filling, but still light. For a taste of the sun, try Mediterranean Fish Soup, served with toasted French bread and Gruyère cheese. To make Chinese Pork Balls & Greens, you bubble the greens briefly in the broth while cooking the pork balls in its steam.

Mexican Vegetable Soup with Tortilla Chips

INGREDIENTS

2 tbsp vegetable or
   extra-virgin olive oil
1 onion, chopped finely
4 garlic cloves, chopped
¼–½ tsp ground cumin
2–3 tsp mild chilli
   powder, such as ancho
   or New Mexico
1 carrot, sliced
1 waxy potato, diced
350 g/12 oz diced fresh
   or canned tomatoes
1 courgette, diced
¼ small cabbage,
   shredded
1 litre/1¾ pints vegetable
   or chicken stock,
   or water
1 corn-on-the-cob, the
   kernels cut off the cob,
   or canned sweetcorn
about 10 green or runner
   beans, topped and
   tailed, and cut into
   2.5 cm/1 inch lengths
salt and pepper

TO SERVE
4–6 tbsp chopped fresh
   coriander
salsa of your choice or
   chopped fresh chilli
tortilla chips

❶ Heat the oil in a heavy-based pan. Add the onion and garlic and cook for a few minutes until softened, then sprinkle in the cumin and chilli powder. Stir in the carrot, potato, tomatoes, courgette and cabbage and cook for 2 minutes, stirring the mixture occasionally.

❷ Pour in the stock. Cover and cook over a medium heat for about 20 minutes, or until the vegetables are tender.

❸ Add extra water if necessary, then stir in the sweetcorn and green beans and cook for another 5–10 minutes, or until the beans are tender. Season with salt and pepper to taste, bearing in mind that the tortilla chips may be salty.

❹ Ladle the soup into soup bowls and sprinkle each portion with fresh coriander. Top with a dab of salsa, then add a handful of tortilla chips.

 extremely easy

 serves 4

 20 minutes

 40 minutes

Beef & Vegetable Soup

INGREDIENTS

225 g/8 oz tomatoes
2 corn-on-the-cobs
1 litre/1¾ pints beef stock
1 carrot, sliced thinly
1 onion, chopped
1–2 small waxy potatoes, diced
¼ cabbage, sliced thinly
¼ tsp ground cumin
¼ tsp mild chilli powder
¼ tsp paprika
225 g/8 oz cooked beef, cut into bite-sized pieces
3–4 tbsp chopped fresh coriander (optional)
hot salsa, to serve

❶ To skin the tomatoes, place in a heatproof bowl, pour boiling water over to cover them, and leave them to stand for 30 seconds. Drain and plunge into cold water. The skins will then slide off easily. Chop the tomatoes.

❷ Using a large knife, cut the corn-on-the-cobs into 2.5 cm/1 inch pieces.

❸ Pour the stock into a pan with the tomatoes, carrot, onion, potatoes and cabbage. Bring to the boil, then reduce the heat and simmer for 10–15 minutes, or until the vegetables are tender.

❹ Add the corn-on-the-cob pieces, the cumin, chilli powder, paprika and beef pieces. Stir well to combine, while bringing back to the boil over a medium heat.

❺ Ladle into soup bowls and serve sprinkled with fresh coriander, if using, with salsa handed round separately.

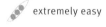 extremely easy

 serves 4

 10 minutes

35–40 minutes

Pozole

INGREDIENTS

450 g/1 lb pork for
    stewing, such as
    lean belly
½ small chicken
about 2 litres/3½ pints
    water
1 chicken stock cube
1 whole garlic bulb,
    divided into cloves
    but not peeled
1 onion, chopped
2 bay leaves
450 g/1 lb canned or
    cooked hominy or
    chickpeas
¼–½ tsp ground cumin
salt and pepper

TO SERVE
½ small cabbage, thinly
    shredded
fried pork skin
dried oregano leaves
dried chilli flakes
tortilla chips
lime wedges

❶ Place the pork and chicken in a large pan. Add enough water to fill the pan. (Do not worry about having too much stock – it will keep for the rest of the week and will last for weeks in the freezer.)

❷ Bring to the boil, then skim off the scum that rises to the surface. Reduce the heat and add the stock cube, garlic, onion and bay leaves to the pan. Simmer, covered, over a medium–low heat until the pork and chicken are both tender and cooked through.

❸ Using a slotted spoon, remove the pork and chicken from the soup and leave to cool. When cool enough to handle, remove the chicken flesh from the bones and cut into small pieces. Then cut the pork into bite-sized pieces. Set the meat aside.

❹ Skim the fat off the soup and discard the bay leaves. Add the hominy or chickpeas and cumin, with salt and pepper to taste. Bring to the boil.

❺ To serve, place a little pork and chicken in soup bowls. Top with cabbage, fried pork skin, oregano and chilli flakes, then spoon the hot soup into the bowls. Serve with tortilla chips and lime wedges.

very easy

serves 4

10 minutes

40 minutes,
plus 10 minutes
to stand

Risi e Bisi

INGREDIENTS

900 g / 2 lb fresh
    unshelled peas
60 g / 2¼ oz unsalted
    butter
1 onion, chopped finely
850 ml / 1½ pints chicken
    stock
200 g / 7 oz arborio rice
2 tbsp chopped fresh
    flat-leaved parsley
60 g / 2¼ oz freshly
    grated Parmesan
    cheese
salt and pepper

TO GARNISH
tomato slices
Parmesan cheese
    shavings
fresh basil leaves

 extremely easy

 serves 4

10–15 minutes

45 minutes

COOK'S TIP
You can substitute
300 g / 10½ oz frozen
peas for fresh: defrost
under running hot water,
add to the softened
onions and cook for 5
minutes with the stock.
Continue from Step 4.

❶ Remove the peas from their shells – the shelled peas should weigh about 300 g / 10½ oz.

❷ Melt the butter in a large heavy-based saucepan over a medium heat. Add the onion and cook for about 2 minutes, stirring occasionally, until they begin to soften.

❸ Add the shelled peas and cook, stirring occasionally, for another 2–3 minutes. Gradually add the chicken stock and bring to the boil. Reduce the heat and simmer, covered, for about 10 minutes, stirring occasionally.

❹ Add the rice and season with a little salt and pepper. Simmer, covered, for about 15 minutes, stirring occasionally, until the rice is just tender.

❺ Stir in the parsley and adjust the seasoning. If the soup is too thick, add a little more stock. Stir in the Parmesan cheese shavings, then ladle the soup into bowls.

❻ Serve immediately, garnished with tomato slices, Parmesan shavings and basil leaves.

Barley & Rice Soup with Chard

INGREDIENTS

100 g / 3½ oz pearl barley
100 g / 3½ oz long-grain brown rice
450 g / 1 lb chard, trimmed and soaked for 10 minutes
2 tbsp olive oil
1 large onion, chopped finely
2 carrots, chopped finely
2 sticks of celery, chopped finely
2 garlic cloves, chopped finely
400 g / 14 oz canned chopped Italian plum tomatoes with their juice
1 bay leaf
1 tsp dried thyme
1 tsp herbes de Provence or dried oregano
1 litre / 1¾ pints chicken or vegetable stock
450 g / 1 lb canned cannellini beans, drained
2 tbsp chopped fresh parsley
salt and pepper
freshly grated Parmesan cheese, to serve

❶ Bring a large saucepan of water to the boil. Add the barley and the brown rice, and return to the boil. Reduce the heat and simmer gently for 30–35 minutes, or until just tender. Drain and set aside.

❷ Drain the chard. Cut out the hard white stems and slice the stems crossways into very thin strips and set aside. Roll the leaves into a cigar shape and shred thinly. Set aside.

❸ Heat the oil in a large saucepan. Add the onion, carrots and celery, and cook, stirring frequently, for about 5 minutes, or until soft and beginning to colour. Add the garlic and cook for a minute longer. Add the tomatoes and their juice, the bay leaf, thyme and herbes de Provence. Reduce the heat and simmer, partially covered, for about 7 minutes, or until all the vegetables are soft.

❹ Stir in the sliced white chard stems and the stock. Simmer gently for about 20 minutes. Add the shredded green chard and simmer for another 15 minutes.

❺ Stir in the beans and parsley with the cooked barley and brown rice. Season with salt and pepper. Bring back to the boil and simmer for another 8–10 minutes. Serve at once with freshly grated Parmesan cheese for sprinkling.

 very easy

 serves 4

 10 minutes

 1 hour, 40 minutes

Turkey & Rice Soup

1 onion, chopped finely
2 carrots, diced
200 g/7 oz long-grain
    white rice
2 leeks, sliced thinly
225 g/8 oz frozen peas
115 g/4 oz fresh or
    defrosted mangetouts,
    sliced thinly
115 g/4 oz fresh spinach
    or watercress, washed
    and shredded
450 g/1 lb cooked turkey
    meat, diced
1 tbsp finely chopped
    fresh parsley
salt and pepper

STOCK
1 bunch fresh parsley
2 turkey legs
1 bay leaf
1 tsp dried thyme
2 onions, unpeeled,
    cut into quarters
2 carrots, cut into chunks
2 sticks of celery, cut into
    chunks
1 parsnip, cut into
    chunks (optional)
1 eating apple or pear
    (optional)
1 tbsp black peppercorns

 easy

 serves 4

 25 minutes

 4 hours

❶ To make the stock, first tie the parsley sprigs into a bundle, then put it into a large pan with the remaining stock ingredients. Pour enough cold water into the pan to cover the ingredients by 2.5 cm/1 inch.

❷ Place the pan on a high heat and bring to the boil, skimming off any foam. Boil for 2 minutes, then reduce the heat to low and simmer very gently for 2–3 hours. Cool the stock slightly, then strain into a large bowl. Skim off any fat from the surface, then wipe a paper towel across it.

❸ Put about 3 litres/5¼ pints of the turkey stock in a large saucepan. Add the onion and carrots and bring to the boil.

❹ Add the rice, reduce the heat and simmer for 15–20 minutes or until the rice is tender, stirring once or twice.

❺ Stir the remaining vegetables into the pan and simmer the soup for 10 minutes. Add the cooked turkey meat, heat the mixture through, and season with salt and pepper. Stir in the parsley and serve the soup hot.

 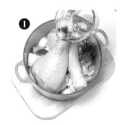 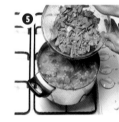

Wild Rice & Smoked Chicken Chowder

INGREDIENTS

75 g/2¾ oz wild rice, washed
3 fresh corn-on-the-cobs, husks and silks removed
2 tbsp vegetable oil
1 large onion, chopped finely
1 stick of celery, sliced thinly
1 leek, trimmed and sliced thinly
½ tsp dried thyme
2 tbsp plain flour
1 litre/1¾ pints chicken stock
250 g/9 oz boned smoked chicken, skinned, diced or shredded
225 ml/8 fl oz double or whipping cream
1 tbsp chopped fresh dill
salt and pepper
fresh dill sprigs, to garnish

❶ Bring a large saucepan of water to the boil. Add a tablespoon of salt and sprinkle in the wild rice. Return to the boil, then reduce the heat and simmer, covered, for about 40 minutes, or until just tender, but still firm to the bite. Do not overcook the rice as it will continue to cook in the soup. Drain and rinse, then set aside.

❷ Hold the corn cobs vertically to a cutting board and, using a sharp, heavy knife, cut down along the cobs to remove the kernels. Set aside the kernels. Scrape the cob to remove the milky juices and reserve them for the soup.

❸ Heat the oil in a large pan over a medium heat. Add the onion, celery, leek and dried thyme. Cook, stirring often, for about 8 minutes, or until the vegetables are very soft.

❹ Sprinkle the flour over the top and stir until blended. Whisk in the stock, a little at a time. Add the corn with any juices. Bring to the boil, skimming off any foam that accumulates. Reduce the heat and simmer for about 25 minutes, or until the vegetables are very soft and tender.

❺ Stir in the smoked chicken, wild rice, cream and dill. Season with salt and pepper. Simmer for 10 minutes, or until the chicken and rice are heated through. Garnish with dill sprigs and serve immediately.

 very easy

 serves 4

 15 minutes

 1½ hours

Green Vegetable Soup with Basil Pesto

INGREDIENTS

1 tbsp olive oil
1 onion, chopped finely
1 large leek, split and
*   sliced thinly*
1 stick of celery, sliced
1 carrot, quartered and
*   sliced thinly*
1 garlic clove, chopped
1.4 litres/2½ pints water
150 g/5½ oz French
*   beans*
1 potato, diced
1 parsnip, diced finely
1 small kohlrabi or
*   turnip, diced*
150 g/5½ oz fresh or
*   defrosted frozen peas*
2 small courgettes,
*   quartered and sliced*
400 g/14 oz canned
*   flageolet beans,*
*   drained and rinsed*
100 g/3½ oz spinach
*   leaves, cut into strips*
salt and pepper

PESTO
1 large garlic clove,
*   chopped very finely*
15 g/½ oz basil leaves
75 g/2¾ oz Parmesan
*   cheese, grated*
4 tbsp virgin olive oil

very easy

serves 4

20 minutes

1 hour

❶ Heat the olive oil in a large saucepan over a medium heat. Add the onion and leek and cook for 5 minutes, stirring occasionally. Add the celery, carrot and garlic and cook, covered, for 5 minutes, stirring frequently,

❷ Cut the French beans into 2.5 cm/1 inch lengths and add them with the water, potato, parsnip, and kohlrabi or turnip. Bring to the boil, reduce the heat to low, and simmer, covered, for 5 minutes.

❸ Add the peas, courgettes and flageolet beans, and season generously with salt and pepper. Cover the pan again and simmer for about 25 minutes, or until all the vegetables are tender.

❹ Meanwhile, make the pesto. Put the garlic, basil and cheese in a food processor with the olive oil, and process until smooth, scraping down the sides. Alternatively, put the ingredients in a mortar and pound them with a pestle.

❺ Add the spinach to the soup and simmer for another 5 minutes. Taste and adjust the seasoning, and stir about 1 tablespoon of the pesto into the soup. Ladle into warm bowls and pass the remaining pesto separately.

Creamy Onion & Broad Bean Soup

INGREDIENTS

1 tbsp butter
2 tsp oil
2 large onions,
   chopped finely
1 leek, sliced thinly
1 garlic clove, crushed
1.2 litres/2 pints water
75 g/2¾ oz white rice
1 bay leaf
½ tsp chopped fresh
   rosemary leaves
½ tsp chopped fresh
   thyme leaves
350 g/12 oz fresh or
   defrosted frozen
   broad beans
100 g/3½ oz rindless
   streaky bacon,
   chopped finely
350 ml/12 fl oz milk,
   plus extra if needed
freshly grated nutmeg
salt and pepper

❶ Heat the butter and half the oil in a large saucepan over a medium heat. Add the onions, leek and garlic. Season with salt and pepper and cook for 10–15 minutes, stirring frequently, until the onion softens.

❷ Add the water, rice, herbs and a large pinch of salt. Bring to the boil, then reduce the heat. Cover and simmer for 15 minutes. Add the broad beans, cover again, and simmer for another 15 minutes, or until the vegetables are tender.

❸ Allow the soup to cool a little, transfer to a blender or a food processor and purée until smooth, working in batches if necessary. (If using a food processor, strain off the liquid and reserve. Purée the soup solids with enough liquid to moisten them, then combine with the remaining liquid.)

❹ Heat the remaining oil in a frying pan over a medium–low heat. Add the bacon and cook until it is crisp, stirring occasionally. Drain on paper towels.

❺ Return the soup to the saucepan and stir in the milk, adding extra if necessary for a thinner soup. Add salt and pepper to taste and a good grating of nutmeg. Simmer for 10 minutes, stirring occasionally. Ladle the soup into bowls and sprinkle with bacon. Serve at once.

 very easy

 serves 4

15 minutes

1 hour,
10 minutes

Shellfish & Tomato Soup

INGREDIENTS

1 kg/2 lb 4 oz mussels
2 tbsp butter
2 shallots, chopped
   finely
4 tbsp plain flour
4 tbsp dry white wine
600 ml/1 pint fish stock
200 g/7 oz queen
   scallops
200 g/7 oz cooked
   peeled prawns
125 ml/4 fl oz double
   cream
4 tomatoes, skinned,
   deseeded and
   chopped
2 tbsp snipped fresh
   chives
juice of ½ lemon, freshly
   squeezed
2 tbsp chopped fresh
   parsley
salt and pepper

❶ Discard any broken mussels and those with open shells that do not close when tapped. Rinse, pull off the beards, and if there are barnacles, scrape them off with a knife under cold running water. Put the mussels in a large, heavy-based saucepan, cover tightly, and cook for 4–5 minutes, or until the mussels open, shaking the pan occasionally.

❷ When they are cool enough to handle, remove the mussels from the shells, adding their additional juices to the cooking liquid. Strain the liquid through a muslin-lined sieve. Top it up with water to make 450 ml/16 fl oz.

❸ Melt the butter in a saucepan over a medium–low heat. Add the shallots and cook for 3–4 minutes, stirring often, until soft. Stir in the flour and cook for 2 minutes. Add the wine.

❹ Slowly add the fish stock and stir well, scraping the pan to mix in the flour. Pour in the mussel cooking liquid and water and bring just to the boil, stirring frequently. Reduce the heat, cover, and simmer for 10 minutes.

❺ Add the scallops, prawns and mussels, and continue to cook for 1 minute. Stir in the cream, tomatoes, chives, lemon juice and parsley. Add salt and more lemon juice to taste. Sprinkle with parsley and serve the soup at once.

easy

serves 4

15 minutes

35 minutes

Chinese Pork Balls & Greens in Broth

INGREDIENTS

2 litres/3½ pints chicken
   stock
85 g/3 oz shiitake
   mushrooms, sliced
   thinly
175 g/6 oz pak choi or
   other Chinese greens,
   sliced into thin
   ribbons
6 spring onions, finely
   sliced
salt and pepper

PORK BALLS

225 g/8 oz lean minced
   pork
25 g/1 oz fresh spinach
   leaves, chopped finely
2 spring onions,
   chopped finely
1 garlic clove, very
   chopped finely
pinch of Chinese 5-spice
   powder
1 tsp soy sauce

❶ To make the pork balls, put the pork, spinach, spring onions and garlic in a bowl. Add the 5-spice powder and soy sauce, and mix until combined.

❷ Shape the pork mixture into 24 balls. Place them in one layer in a steamer that will fit over the top of a saucepan.

❸ Bring the stock just to the boil in a saucepan that will accommodate the steamer. Regulate the heat so that the liquid bubbles gently. Add the mushrooms to the stock and place the steamer, covered, on top of the pan. Steam for 10 minutes. Remove the steamer and set aside on a plate.

❹ Add the pak choi or greens and spring onions to the pan and cook gently in the stock for 3–4 minutes, or until the leaves are wilted. Taste the soup and adjust the seasoning, adding salt and pepper if necessary.

❺ Divide the pork balls evenly among 6 warm bowls and ladle the soup over them. Serve at once.

 very easy

serves 4

15 minutes

25 minutes

Green Lentil, Potato & Ham Soup

INGREDIENTS

300 g/10½ oz Puy lentils
2 tsp butter
1 large onion,
    chopped finely
2 carrots, chopped finely
1 garlic clove,
    chopped finely
450 ml/16 fl oz water
1 bay leaf
¼ tsp dried sage or
    rosemary
1 litre/1¾ pints chicken
    stock
225 g/8 oz potatoes,
    diced (see Cook's Tip)
1 tbsp tomato purée
115 g/4 oz smoked ham,
    diced finely
chopped fresh parsley,
    to garnish

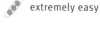 extremely easy

 serves 4

10–15 minutes

55 minutes

❶ Rinse and drain the lentils, check for any small stones and remove them.

❷ Melt the butter in a large saucepan or a flameproof casserole over a medium heat. Add the onion, carrots and garlic, cover, and cook for 4–5 minutes, or until the onion is slightly softened, stirring frequently.

❸ Add the lentils to the vegetables with the water, bay leaf, and sage or rosemary. Bring to the boil, reduce the heat, cover, and simmer for 10 minutes.

❹ Add the stock, potatoes, tomato purée and ham. Bring back to a simmer. Cover and continue simmering for 25–30 minutes, or until the vegetables are tender.

❺ Season to taste with salt and pepper and remove the bay leaf. Ladle the soup into warm bowls, garnish with parsley, and serve immediately.

COOK'S TIP

Cut the potatoes into small dice, about 5 mm/¼ inch, so they will be in proportion with the lentils.

64

Pumpkin & Coconut Soup

INGREDIENTS

1 kg/2 lb 4 oz pumpkin
1 tbsp groundnut oil
1 tsp yellow mustard
    seeds
1 garlic clove, crushed
1 large onion, chopped
1 stick of celery, chopped
1 small red chilli,
    chopped
850 ml/1½ pints stock
1 tbsp dried prawns
5 tbsp coconut cream
salt and pepper
extra coconut cream,
    to garnish

❶ Halve the pumpkin and remove the seeds. Cut away the skin and dice the flesh.

❷ Heat the oil in a large flameproof casserole and fry the mustard seeds until they begin to pop. Stir in the garlic, onion, celery and chilli, and stir-fry for 1–2 minutes.

❸ Add the diced pumpkin with the stock and dried prawns, and bring to the boil. Lower the heat, cover, and simmer gently for about 30 minutes, or until all the ingredients are very tender.

❹ Transfer the mixture to a food processor or a blender, and process until smooth. Return the mixture to the pan and stir in the coconut cream.

❺ Adjust the seasoning to taste with salt and pepper and serve hot, decorating each bowl with coconut cream.

 very easy

 serves 4

 20 minutes

 45 minutes

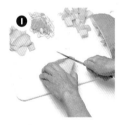

COOK'S TIP

For an extra touch of garnish, swirl a spoon of thick coconut milk into each bowl of soup as you serve it.

Cullen Skink

INGREDIENTS

225 g/8 oz smoked
    haddock fillet
2 tbsp butter
1 onion, chopped finely
600 ml/1 pint milk
350 g/12 oz potatoes,
    cut into dice
350 g/12 oz cod, boned,
    skinned and cubed
150 ml/5 fl oz double
    cream
2 tbsp chopped fresh
    parsley
lemon juice, to taste
salt and pepper

TO GARNISH
lemon slices
parsley sprigs

❶ Put the haddock fillet in a large frying pan and cover with boiling water. Leave for 10 minutes. Drain the fish, reserving 225 ml/8 fl oz of the soaking water. Flake the fillets, taking care to remove all the bones.

❷ Heat the butter in a large saucepan and add the onion. Cook gently for 10 minutes, or until softened. Add the milk and bring to a gentle simmer before adding the diced potato. Cook for 10 minutes.

❸ Add the reserved haddock flakes and cod. Simmer for an additional 10 minutes, or until the cod is tender.

❹ Remove about one-third of the fish and potatoes, put in a food processor and blend until smooth. Alternatively, push through a sieve into a bowl. Return to the soup with the cream, parsley and seasoning. Taste and add a little lemon juice, if desired. Add a little of the soaking water if the soup seems too thick. Reheat gently and serve at once.

 very easy

 serves 4

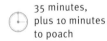 20 minutes

35 minutes,
plus 10 minutes
to poach

COOK'S TIP
Use Finnan haddock,
if available, rather
than yellow-dyed
haddock fillet, which
is often not haddock
but whiting.

Mediterranean Fish Soup

INGREDIENTS

1 kg/2 lb 4 oz mixed fish
2 tbsp olive oil
1 bulb fennel, trimmed
  and chopped
2 shallots, chopped
2 garlic cloves, chopped
600 g/1 lb 4 oz sun-
  ripened tomatoes,
  chopped
1 bouquet garni of
  2 sprigs fresh
  flat-leaved parsley,
  2 sprigs fresh thyme
  and 1 bay leaf, tied in
  a 7.5 cm/3 inch piece
  of celery
pinch of saffron threads
700 ml/1¼ pints chilled
  fish stock
salt and pepper
French Pastis or other
  aniseed-flavoured
  liqueur (optional)

TO SERVE
commercially made
  rouille
1 loaf French bread,
  sliced and toasted
125 g/4½ oz Gruyère
  cheese, grated

❶ To prepare the fish, remove any skin and bones, and chop.

❷ Heat the oil in a heavy-based pan. Add the fennel and cook for 5 minutes, stirring frequently. Add the shallots and garlic and cook for about 5 minutes, or until the shallots are soft and the fennel is tender.

❸ Stir in the mixed fish and add the tomatoes, bouquet garni, saffron, fish stock and salt and pepper to taste.

❹ Bring the soup almost to the boil, stirring occasionally. Lower the heat, partially cover, and simmer for 30 minutes, stirring occasionally to break up the tomatoes. Skim the surface as necessary.

❺ Remove the bouquet garni. Process the soup in a food processor until it is smooth, then work it through a food mill into a large bowl.

❻ Return to the rinsed-out pan and heat without boiling. Adjust the seasoning. Stir in a little Pastis, if using.

❼ Spread the rouille on the toast. Sprinkle the cheese on top. Place equal amounts of toast in each bowl and ladle the hot soup over them. Serve the soup at once, while hot.

easy

serves 4

30 minutes

1 hour

Provençal Pumpkin Winter Soup

INGREDIENTS

1 kg / 2 lb 4 oz fresh orange-fleshed pumpkin or winter squash, such as butternut or hubbard
2 tbsp olive oil
1 large onion, chopped
2 garlic cloves, chopped
2 tsp fresh thyme leaves
1.5 litres / 2¾ pints chicken or vegetable stock, or water
1 bay leaf
½ tsp crushed dried chillies
100 g / 3½ oz short-grain rice, such as arborio or Valencia
1 tsp salt
300 ml / 10 fl oz single cream or milk
freshly grated nutmeg
pepper
fresh thyme sprigs, to garnish
garlic croûtons, to serve (optional)

❶ Remove any seeds from the pumpkin, then peel. Cut into small cubes and set aside.

❷ Heat the oil in a large saucepan over a medium heat. Add the onion and cook for about 4 minutes, or until soft.

❸ Stir in the garlic and thyme and cook for 1 minute. Stir in the pumpkin, stock, bay leaf, chillies and half the rice. Bring to the boil, skimming off any foam. Reduce the heat to low and simmer, covered, for about 1 hour, or until the pumpkin is very tender.

❹ Meanwhile, bring a pan of water to the boil. Add the salt, sprinkle in the remaining rice and simmer for 15 minutes, or until tender. Drain the rice, rinse it thoroughly, drain again, and set it aside.

❺ Working in batches, process the pumpkin soup in a blender until it is smooth, and strain it into a large saucepan. Add the cooked rice, cream and nutmeg to taste. Season with salt and pepper and garnish with thyme sprigs. Serve the soup hot, sprinkled with croûtons.

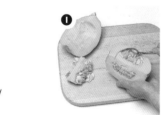

very easy

serves 4

15 minutes

1 hour, 20 minutes

Cauliflower & Cider Soup

INGREDIENTS

25 g/1 oz butter
1 onion, chopped finely
1 garlic clove, crushed
1 carrot, sliced thinly
500 g/1 lb 2 oz
*   cauliflower florets*
*   (from 1 medium head)*
600 ml/1 pint dry cider
freshly grated nutmeg
125 ml/4 fl oz milk
125 ml/4 fl oz double
*   cream*
salt and pepper
snipped chives,
*   to garnish*

very easy

serves 4

15 minutes

1¼ hours

COOK'S TIP
Instead of dry cider, you can use 125 ml/ 4 fl oz each of white wine, apple juice and water.

❶ Melt the butter in a saucepan over a medium heat. Add the onion and garlic and cook for about 5 minutes, stirring occasionally, until just softened.

❷ Add the carrot and cauliflower to the pan and pour the cider over them. Season with salt, pepper and a generous grating of nutmeg. Bring to the boil, then reduce the heat to low. Cover, and cook gently for about 50 minutes, or until the vegetables are very soft.

❸ Allow the soup to cool slightly, then transfer to a blender or a food processor and process until smooth, working in batches if necessary. (If using a food processor, strain off the cooking liquid and reserve. Purée the soup solids with enough cooking liquid to moisten them, then combine with the remaining liquid.)

❹ Return the soup to the saucepan and stir in the milk and cream. Taste and adjust the seasoning, if necessary. Simmer the soup over a low heat, stirring occasionally, until heated through.

❺ Ladle the soup into warm bowls, garnish with chives, and serve hot.

Special Occasions

There may be times when you want to serve a soup that is really out of the ordinary, especially if you are planning a theme evening. For a Mexican meal, for example, Yucatecan Citrus Soup, with charred onions, garlic, and the rind and juice of mixed citrus fruits, will hit the right note, and to accompany a Chinese meal try the classic Chinese Crab & Sweetcorn Soup. Trout & Celeriac Soup and Lemon Veal Soup with Mushrooms both give an impression of quiet elegance, and are perfect for a special lunch or dinner.

Creamy Sweetcorn Soup with Egg

INGREDIENTS

1 tbsp vegetable oil
3 garlic cloves, crushed
1 tsp fresh ginger root, grated
700 ml/1¼ pints chicken stock
375 g/13 oz canned creamed sweetcorn
1 tbsp Thai fish sauce
175 g/6 oz canned white crab meat, drained
1 egg
salt and pepper
fresh coriander, shredded, and paprika, to garnish

❶ Heat the oil in a large saucepan and fry the garlic for 1 minute, stirring constantly.

❷ Add the ginger to the pan, then stir in the stock and creamed sweetcorn. Bring to the boil.

❸ Stir in the fish sauce, crab meat and salt and pepper, then return the soup to the boil.

❹ Beat the egg, then stir lightly into the soup so that it sets into long strands. Simmer gently for about 30 seconds, or until the egg is just set.

❺ Ladle the soup into bowls and serve hot, garnished with shredded coriander and pepper sprinkled over the surface.

 extremely easy

 serves 4

5 minutes

20 minutes

Chinese Crab & Sweetcorn Soup

INGREDIENTS

1 tbsp vegetable oil
1 small onion,
    chopped finely
1 garlic clove,
    chopped finely
1 tsp grated fresh ginger
1 small red chilli,
    deseeded and
    chopped finely
2 tbsp Chinese rice wine
    or dry sherry
225 g/8 oz fresh white
    crab meat
315 g/11 oz canned
    sweetcorn, drained
600 ml/1 pint light
    chicken stock
1 tbsp light soy sauce
2 tbsp chopped
    coriander
2 eggs, beaten
salt and pepper
1 red bird's eye chilli,
    to garnish (optional)

❶ Heat the oil in a large saucepan and add the onion. Cook gently for 5 minutes, or until softened. Add the garlic, ginger and chilli and cook for an additional minute.

❷ Add the rice wine or sherry, and bubble until reduced by half. Add the crab meat, sweetcorn, chicken stock and soy sauce. Bring to the boil and simmer gently for 5 minutes. Stir in the coriander. Season to taste.

❸ Remove from the heat and pour in the eggs. Wait for a few seconds and then stir well to break the eggs into ribbons. Serve immediately, perhaps garnished with a red bird's eye chilli cut into a tassel.

 extremely easy

 serves 4

5–10 minutes

25 minutes

Creamy Scallop Soup

INGREDIENTS

50 g/2 oz butter
1 onion, chopped finely
450 g/1 lb potatoes,
  diced
600 ml/1 pint hot
  fish stock
350 g/12 oz prepared
  scallops, including
  corals if available
350 ml/12 fl oz milk
2 egg yolks
125 ml/4 fl oz double
  cream
salt and pepper
1 tbsp chopped fresh
  parsley, to garnish

easy

serves 4

20 minutes

40 minutes

COOK'S TIP
For convenience, you could use canned crab meat. Make sure it is well drained before adding it to the soup.

❶ Melt the butter in a large saucepan over a gentle heat. Add the onion and cook very gently for 10 minutes, or until the onion is softened but not coloured. Add the potatoes and seasoning, cover, and cook for another 10 minutes over a very low heat.

❷ Pour on the hot fish stock, bring to the boil and simmer for 10–15 minutes, or until the potatoes are tender.

❸ Meanwhile, prepare the scallops. If you have the corals, chop them coarsely and set them aside. Chop the white meat coarsely and put in a second saucepan with the milk. Bring to a gentle simmer and cook for 6–8 minutes, or until the scallops are just tender.

❹ When the potatoes are cooked, transfer them and their cooking liquid to a food processor or a blender and blend to a purée. Alternatively, press through a nylon sieve. Return the mixture to a clean saucepan with the scallops and their milk and the pieces of coral, if using.

❺ Whisk together the egg yolks and cream, then take the pan off the heat and add them to the soup. Return the pan to a very gentle heat and reheat, stirring constantly, until it thickens slightly. Do not boil or the soup will curdle. Season to taste and serve at once, sprinkled with fresh parsley.

Yucatecan Citrus Soup

INGREDIENTS

2 onions
15 large garlic cloves,
    unpeeled
1 tbsp extra-virgin
    olive oil
1.3 litres/2¼ pints
    vegetable, chicken
    or fish stock
225 ml/8 fl oz water
8 ripe tomatoes, diced
pinch of dried oregano
1 fresh green chilli, such
    as jalapeño or
    serrano, deseeded
    and chopped
pinch of ground cumin
½ tsp finely grated
    grapefruit rind
½ tsp finely grated
    lime rind
½ tsp finely grated
    orange rind
juice and diced flesh
    of 2 limes
juice of 1 orange
juice of 1 grapefruit
salt and pepper

TO GARNISH
tortilla chips, or sliced
    tortilla strips fried
    until crisp
2 tbsp chopped fresh
    coriander

 very easy

 serves 4

15 minutes

45 minutes

❶ Cut one unpeeled onion in half. Peel the other and chop it very finely.

❷ Heat a large heavy-based frying pan, add the unpeeled onion halves and garlic, and cook over a medium–high heat until the skins char and the onions are caramelized on their cut sides; the garlic should be soft on the inside. Remove from the pan and allow to cool slightly.

❸ Meanwhile, heat the oil in a pan and sauté the remaining onion lightly until soft. Add the stock and water, and bring to the boil. Reduce the heat and simmer for a few minutes.

❹ Peel the charred onion and garlic, then chop roughly and add to the simmering soup, together with the tomatoes, oregano, chilli and cumin. Cook for about 15 minutes, stirring the soup occasionally.

❺ Add the citrus rind, season with salt and pepper, then simmer for another 2 minutes. Remove from the heat and stir in the lime flesh and citrus juices.

❻ Ladle into soup bowls, garnish with tortilla chips and fresh coriander, and serve.

Mexican Fish & Roasted Tomato Soup

INGREDIENTS

5 ripe tomatoes
5 garlic cloves, unpeeled
500 g/1 lb 2 oz snapper, cut into chunks
1 litre/1¾ pints fish stock, or water, plus a fish stock cube or two
2–3 tbsp olive oil
1 onion, chopped
2 fresh chillies, such as serrano, deseeded and sliced thinly in rounds
lime wedges, to serve

❶ Heat an ungreased heavy-based frying pan, add the whole tomatoes and garlic and char over a high heat or under a preheated grill. The skins of the vegetables should blacken and char, and the flesh inside should be tender. Alternatively, place the tomatoes and garlic cloves in a roasting tin and bake in a preheated oven at 190–200°C/375–400°F/Gas Mark 5–6 for about 40 minutes.

❷ Leave the tomatoes and garlic to cool, then remove the skins and chop coarsely, combining them with any juices from the pan. Set aside.

❸ Poach the snapper in the stock over a medium heat just until it is opaque and quite firm. Remove the fish from the heat and set aside.

❹ Heat the oil in a pan and cook the chopped onion until softened. Strain in the cooking liquid from the fish, then add the roughly chopped tomatoes and garlic, and stir.

❺ Bring to the boil, then reduce the heat and simmer for about 5 minutes to combine the flavours. Add the chillies.

❻ Divide chunks of the poached fish between soup bowls, ladle the hot soup over the fish and serve with lime wedges for squeezing over the top.

easy

serves 4

10 minutes

1 hour, 10 minutes

Chicken, Avocado & Chipotle Soup

INGREDIENTS

1.5 litres/2¾ pints
   chicken stock
2–3 garlic cloves,
   chopped finely
1–2 chipotle chillies, cut
   into very thin strips
1 avocado
lime or lemon juice,
   for tossing
3–5 spring onions,
   sliced thinly
350–400 g/12–14 oz
   cooked chicken breast
   meat, torn or cut into
   shreds or thin strips
2 tbsp chopped fresh
   coriander

TO SERVE
1 lime, cut into wedges
handful of tortilla chips
   (optional)

❶ Place the stock in a pan with the garlic and chipotle chillies, and bring to the boil.

❷ Meanwhile, cut the avocado in half around the stone. Twist apart, then remove the stone with a knife. Carefully peel off the skin, dice the flesh and toss in lime or lemon juice to prevent discoloration.

❸ Arrange the spring onions, chicken, avocado and fresh coriander in the base of 4 soup bowls or alternatively spoon them into a large serving bowl.

❹ Ladle hot stock over the top, and serve the soup with lime and a handful of tortilla chips.

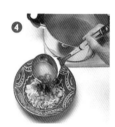

 extremely easy

 serves 4

15 minutes

10–15 minutes

Trout & Celeriac Soup

INGREDIENTS

700 g/1 lb 9 oz whole
   trout
200 g/7 oz celeriac,
   peeled and diced
50 ml/2 fl oz double
   cream
3 tbsp cornflour,
   dissolved in
   3 tbsp water
chopped fresh chervil or
   parsley, to garnish

FISH STOCK BASE
1 tbsp butter
1 onion, sliced thinly
1 carrot, sliced thinly
1 leek, sliced thinly
225 ml/8 fl oz dry white
   wine
1.2 litres/2 pints water
1 bay leaf

❶ For the fish stock base, melt the butter in a fish kettle, a saucepan or a cast-iron casserole. Add the onion, carrot and leek and cook for 3 minutes, or until the onion starts to soften. Add the wine, water and bay leaf. Bring to the boil, reduce the heat a little, cover, and boil gently for 15 minutes.

❷ Add the fish (if necessary, cut the fish into pieces to fit). Bring back to the boil and skim off any foam rising to the top. Reduce the heat and simmer gently for 20 minutes.

❸ Remove the fish and set aside. Strain the stock through a muslin-lined sieve into a clean saucepan. Remove any fat from the stock. (There should be about 1.5 litres/2¾ pints stock.) Bring the stock to the boil. Add the celeriac and boil gently, uncovered, for 15–20 minutes, or until it is tender and the liquid has reduced by one-third.

❹ When the fish is cool enough to handle, peel off the skin and remove the flesh from the bones. Discard the skin, bones, head and tail.

❺ Add the cream to the soup and when it comes back to the boil, stir in the cornflour. Boil gently for 2–3 minutes, or until slightly thickened, stirring frequently. Return the fish to the soup. Cook for 3–4 minutes to reheat. Season to taste and serve garnished with chervil or parsley.

easy

serves 4

20 minutes

1½ hours

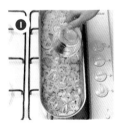

Lemon Veal Soup with Mushrooms

INGREDIENTS

350 g/12 oz boneless veal, cut into 1 cm/ ½ inch pieces
1 litre/1¾ pints chicken stock
1 onion, quartered
2 carrots, sliced thinly
2 garlic cloves, halved
1 pared strip lemon rind
1 bay leaf
1 tbsp butter
350 g/12 oz small button mushrooms, quartered
4 tbsp cornflour
125 ml/4 fl oz double cream
freshly grated nutmeg
fresh lemon juice, to taste (optional)
1–2 tbsp chopped fresh parsley
salt and pepper

❶ Put the veal in a large saucepan and add the stock. Bring just to the boil and skim off any foam rising to the surface.

❷ Add the onion, carrots, garlic, lemon rind and bay leaf. Season with salt and pepper. Reduce the heat and simmer, partially covered, for about 45 minutes, stirring occasionally, until the veal is very tender.

❸ Remove the veal and carrots with a slotted spoon and reserve, covered. Strain the stock into a clean saucepan. Discard the onion and garlic, lemon rind and bay leaf.

❹ Melt the butter in a frying pan over a medium–high heat. Add the mushrooms, season, and fry gently until lightly golden. Reserve with the veal and carrots.

❺ Mix together the cornflour and cream. Bring the cooking liquid to the boil and whisk in the cream mixture. Boil gently for 2–3 minutes until it thickens, whisking almost constantly.

❻ Add the reserved meat and vegetables to the soup and simmer over a low heat for about 5 minutes, or until heated through. Taste and adjust the seasoning, adding nutmeg and a squeeze of lemon juice, if wished. Stir in the parsley, then ladle into warm bowls and serve.

easy

serves 4

15 minutes

1 hour

Iced Salsa Soup

INGREDIENTS

2 large corn-on-the-cobs,
    or 225 g/8 oz frozen
    sweetcorn kernels
1 tbsp olive oil
1 orange or red pepper,
    cored, deseeded and
    chopped finely
1 green pepper, cored,
    deseeded and
    chopped finely
1 sweet onion, such as
    Vidalia, chopped finely
3 ripe tomatoes,
    skinned, deseeded
    and chopped
½ tsp chilli powder,
    or to taste
125 ml/4 fl oz water
450 ml/16 fl oz tomato
    juice
chilli purée (optional)
salt and pepper

TO GARNISH
3–4 spring onions,
    chopped finely
fresh coriander

❶ Cut the corn kernels from the cobs, or if using frozen sweetcorn, defrost and drain.

❷ Heat the oil in a saucepan over a medium–high heat. Add the peppers and cook, stirring briskly, for 3 minutes. Add the onion and continue cooking for about 2 minutes, or until it starts to colour slightly.

❸ Add the tomatoes, sweetcorn and chilli powder, and continue cooking, stirring frequently, for 1 minute. Pour in the water and when it bubbles, reduce the heat, cover, and cook for another 4–5 minutes, or until the peppers are just barely tender.

❹ Transfer the mixture to a large container and stir in the tomato juice. Season with salt and pepper and add more chilli powder if wished. Cover and refrigerate until cold.

❺ Taste and adjust the seasoning. For a more spicy soup, stir in a little chilli purée to taste. For a thinner soup, add a small amount of iced water. Ladle into chilled bowls and garnish with spring onions and fresh coriander leaves.

extremely easy

serves 4

15 minutes,
plus 3–4 hours
to chill

20 minutes

barley & rice soup with
    chard 50
beef & vegetable soup 44

cauliflower & cider
    soup 74
celeriac, leek & potato
    soup 22
celery soups
    barley & rice soup 50
    chicken soup with stars 28
    prawn bisque with rice 12
    wild rice & smoked
        chicken chowder 54
chicken soups
    chicken, avocado &
        chipotle soup 88
    chicken soup with stars 28
    wild rice & smoked
        chicken chowder 54
chilled garlic & almond
    soup 16
Chinese crab & sweetcorn
    soup 80
Chinese pork balls & greens
    in broth 62
citrus soup 84
cold cucumber & smoked
    salmon soup 34
courgettes
    courgette soup with rice
        & lime 10
    Mexican vegetable soup 42
creamy soups
    onion & broad bean
        soup 58
    scallop soup 82
    sweetcorn soup with
        egg 78
cullen skink 68

egg & lemon soup 14

fish & shellfish soup
    Chinese crab & sweetcorn
        soup 80
    cold cucumber & smoked
        salmon soup 34
    creamy scallop soup 82
    cullen skink 68
    Mediterranean soup 70
    Mexican fish & roasted
        tomato soup 86
    trout & celeriac soup 90

garlic & almond soup 16
gazpacho 8, 30
Greek egg & lemon soup 14
green lentil, potato &
    ham soup 64
green vegetable soup
    with basil pesto 56

iced salsa soup 94

leek soups
    celeriac, leek & potato
        soup 22
    sweet potato, apple &
        leek soup 26
lemon veal soup with
    mushrooms 92
lentil, potato & ham soup 64

Mediterranean fish soup 70
melon gazpacho 30
Mexican dishes
    fish & roasted tomato
        soup 86
    vegetable soup with
        tortilla chips 42
mushroom & tofu broth 36

onion & broad bean soup 58

pasta soups
    chicken soup with stars 28
pea soup 24
pepper soups
    pepper & tomato soup
        with dill 18
    spicy gazpacho 8
pork soups
    Chinese pork balls
        & greens in broth 62
    pozole 46
potato soups
    beef & vegetable soup 44
    celeriac, leek & potato
        soup 22
    green lentil, potato &
        ham soup 64
    watercress Vichyssoise 32
pozole 46
prawn bisque with rice 12

Provençal pumpkin winter
    soup 72
pumpkin & coconut soup 66

rice soups
    barley & rice soup with
        chard 50
    prawn bisque 12
    risi e bisi 48
    spicy courgette soup with
        rice & lime 10
    tarragon pea soup 24
    turkey & rice soup 52
    wild rice & smoked
        chicken chowder 54
risi e bisi 48
roasted pepper & tomato
    soup with dill 18

shellfish & tomato soup 60
spicy soups
    courgette soup with rice
        & lime 10
    gazpacho 8
    iced salsa 94
spinach soup 20
sweet & sour cabbage
    soup 38
sweet potato, apple & leek
    soup 26
sweetcorn soup with egg 78

tarragon pea soup 24
trout & celeriac soup 90
turkey & rice soup 52

vegetable soups
    barley and rice soup with
        chard 50
    green vegetable soup with
        basil pesto 56
    onion and broad bean soup
        58
    Provencal pumpkin soup 72
    pumpkin and coconut 66
    risi e bisi 48
    Vichyssoise 32

watercress Vichyssoise 32
wild rice & smoked
    chicken chowder 54

Yucatecan citrus soup 84